TO LEARN THE FUTURE:
POEMS FOR TEACHERS

To Learn the Future

EDITED BY

Jane Cooper

Lilias Fraser

Kate Hendry

Scottish **Poetry** Library

First published in 2018
by the Scottish Poetry Library
5 Crichton's Close
Edinburgh
EH8 8DT
www.scottishpoetrylibrary.org.uk

ISBN 978-1-9999806-0-3

The publisher is grateful for partner support and individual
donations towards the costs of this anthology.

Typeset in Stone Print and Carter Sans by Gerry Cambridge
www.gerrycambridge.com
Produced by Productive Production, www.productive.uk.com

Printed and bound in Scotland

CONTENTS

SECTION III: BALANCING IT ALL

LINES FOR A BOOKMARK   *Gael Turnbull*

You who read...
May you seek
As you look;
May you keep
What you need;
May you care
What you choose;
And know here
In this book
Something strange,
Something sure,
That will change
You and be yours.

All our lives we remember our teachers. A good teacher knows it is not lessons they teach but students. This gem of a book is for everyone, and I hope it will be enjoyed as much by the PE and Physics teachers as by those who deliver *A Midsummer Night's Dream*. Here are texts that talk to each other and to the reader—you, dear teacher—using the language of poetry to investigate, to remember and to celebrate education. Whether you savour them in your lunch hour or after hours, these poems will hold open the door and make you welcome.

The wonderful thing about this book is that it has no agenda, no policy directive. No grading required. No planning necessary. What a relief! Poems to bounce off, to inspire, to offer moments of recognition, a necessary pause. Poems to ring through good days and bad. These poems are not teaching aids, but life aids; not set texts but subtexts. This gift is not homework but heart work. Please turn over the page and begin!

Jackie Kay
Scottish Makar

FROM THE EDITORS

In 2014, the Scottish Poetry Library published *Tools of the Trade*, a friendly, pocket-sized book of poems for new doctors. The day after its launch, Jane Cooper asked when there would be a similar anthology for teachers. The answer is 'now', and this is that book.

Whether you're stepping into your first classroom, or looking back on decades of pupils, colleagues, marking and admin, this book is for you. We hope you will find a poem that speaks to you, or that tells you what you are thinking is perfectly normal, or that reminds you why this job is so precious and vital.

We looked for poems to reflect some of the range of voices and experiences in Scotland's classrooms and staffrooms. Where possible, we've included original languages as well as translations; in other cases, the original language is English but the poem explores a richness of cultural identity. We have retained the American English spellings in poems where they are used.

Editing a book with a purpose like this makes us aware of how many people value teaching and teachers; we'd like to thank all the people who have been so generous with time, ideas and contacts.

We're very grateful in particular to the librarians of the Scottish Poetry Library, and to Hamish Whyte, whose ingenious searches provided a wealth of poems; and to the poets and publishers who generously gave permission to use poems and wrote welcoming notes for readers. Megan Volpert and

Bryan Borland provided delightful email help in connection with poems from *This Assignment Is So Gay* (Sibling Rivalry Press), and Gregory Woods and Hugh Thomson helped us finally decide on a title. We were glad to have Gerry Cambridge as our designer and typesetter, and Robyn Marsack to see the book through the press.

The book is the better for all this, and for the help of teachers and education professionals from Scotland, with their various teaching specialisms and years of service, who are listed at the end of the book.

We are proud that this book is supported by professional education organisations, including the General Teaching Council of Scotland, and teaching unions including the significant support of Educational Institute of Scotland (EIS), and the Scottish Secondary Teachers' Association (SSTA), the National Association of Schoolmasters and Union of Women Teachers (NASUWT) and the Association of Headteachers and Deputes Scotland (AHDS). Their enthusiasm, interest and care for the project has been considerable. You will find more details about these organisations at the back of the book: they, like this book of poems, are here for you at every stage of your teaching career.

Jane Cooper
Secondary teacher

Lilias Fraser
Scottish Poetry Library

Kate Hendry
Secondary teacher

I

STARTING OUT

THE DOOR *Miroslav Holub*

Go and open the door.
     Maybe outside there's
     a tree, or a wood,
     a garden,
     or a magic city.

Go and open the door.
     Maybe a dog's rummaging.
     Maybe you'll see a face,
or an eye,
or the picture
     of a picture.

Go and open the door.
     If there's a fog
     it will clear.

Go and open the door.
     Even if there's only
     the darkness ticking,
     even if there's only
     the hollow wind,
     even if
          nothing
               is there,
go and open the door.

At least
there'll be
a draught.

*Translated from Czech by Ian Milner, who also translated
the poem by Holub on p. 35*

ODE TO TEACHERS *Pat Mora*

I remember
the first day,
how I looked down,
hoping you wouldn't see
me,
and when I glanced up,
I saw your smile
shining like a soft light
from deep inside you.

'I'm listening,' you encourage us.
'Come on!
Join our conversation,
let us hear your neon certainties,
thorny doubts, tangled angers,'
but for weeks I hid inside.

I read and reread your notes
praising
my writing,
and you whispered,
'We need you
and your stories
and questions
that like a fresh path
will take us to new vistas.'

Slowly, your faith grew
into my courage
and for you—
instead of handing you
a note or apple or flowers—
I raised my hand.

I carry your smile
and faith inside like I carry
my dog's face,
my sister's laugh,
creamy melodies,
the softness of sunrise,
steady blessings of stars,
autumn smell of gingerbread,
the security of a sweater on a chilly day.

HOW TO BE A TEACHER *Rebecca Lynne Fullan*

First,
despair of what you know.
It will not be enough.
It is not the right kind.
You are as unprepared
as you fear.

Let the things you know
fall out of your hands
and shatter on the floor.
They will not fall
in neat pieces
but blow away instantly
in dust.

This dust will coat your hands,
your students' faces. It will get
into your lungs and make you cough.
It will get into your eyes, where it sparkles
and refracts.

Bring stories in your open hands.
There will be questions like, what
is a devil? How many quotes
are we required to use? Do you want
a revolution? Would you, personally, go
to the site of one? When is that essay due,
again, and what is it about?

When one of them tells you he cannot write,
ask him to draw. And when he draws a fish,
look at the fish. And when he writes about the fish,
take what you know about him now, as mysterious
as what you did not know before, and hold it.

Love your students. Surprise and disappoint
them. They will do the same for you.
They will write you on New Year's Eve.
One will send a picture of her bandaged head.
One will send an essay for revision.
One will ask you, do you understand how I feel?

Take what you know now and hold it close.
Make it into pottery, something beautiful.
Next time you begin a class, hold it in your hands
on the very first day, when you wish
you were a plumber or a politician or
anything but this—and let it drop.
And so begin.

*I love the way this poem suggests that knowledge is created in
collaboration. In this particular American context, students
may be older and teaching contact different; but the sense of
shared discovery and learning is the same for all of us. We learn
how to teach through and with our pupils—acknowledging
what we don't know, building answers together. For me, the joy*

of teaching is in building relationships and this poem captures the rewards, surprises and challenges of that process. We learn to handle unexpected questions and confidences with a boundaried empathy.

—Secondary English teacher, Edinburgh

FEAR OF THE LITANY *Maggie Kazel*

I remember thinking I teach every grade
every classroom that means eventually
I'm supposed to know every name.
How the hell do I do that?

I ask some other teachers.
No one has any tricks, they just say oh,
you'll get the hang of it, you will.

But that's because maybe I look like a teacher,
or a smart person, or adult enough to handle it.
I'm faking it, I can't do this, I've got them
all faked out.

Barely the end of September,
and Terry sees me kissing her
before I get out of the car.
Now I have to deal with this.
I may want to work here longer
than the end of the pay period.
Shit. So I go in, and I
wait till the end of the day.

Yeah, I saw you with her.
She's my lover.
Yeah, well I figured she wasn't just a good friend,
since my wife kisses me goodbye on the lips,
not my friends.

He was already being himself, Terry, teasing.
So I blurted it out, my fear of the litany
of names, my fear of faking
being a teacher and he said
Oh but you are.
You're right for this place and
you're right on schedule, breaking down.
You've got it, I've watched you with them.

What about technique, philosophy, content?
You might want to get your kiss
before the parking lot,
but even that...they trust you.
That's all it takes.

RAISING THEIR HANDS *Julia Lisella*

Sometimes I dream about my students,
the pink of their palms
red and raw.
One student, seven feet tall,
his long back
hunched over the desk,
his arm out and above him—
he could be waving
or stopping a train.
Another student wears eyeliner for the stage.
She bends from the ribs,
her body forming a tiny "c,"
her hand up sudden as a whitecap.

Some days they frighten me.
Put your hands down, I tell them.
Shout. Explode. Scream it.
Instead they look at me and smile
the way they would at foreigners who don't speak the language.
That's how they've trained me.
Now I wait until I see a scatter of fingers
and then I choose—
Yes, your palm, your hand,
your arched spine,
you with your idea,
Speak.

It's perfectly understandable to want our students to shout with excitement, to share in our enthusiasm for a subject or lesson. The challenge is when they don't. The reward is when the one who is hunched over, seemingly oblivious, lifts their head, raises their hand, and shares what they find exciting.

Ernesto L. Abeytia, poet, writer and university teacher, USA

When I first started teaching, I thought
my students could see my heart on my sleeve.
I thought they could read the footnotes of
a body splayed open as a book.
I felt embarrassed to have such a
visible heart; there was something shameful about
the whole goopy mess, its ungovernable pulsations,
its lightning blush. It seemed none of my students
had a heart like mine; their hearts were bundled
in their baggy sweatshirts like a packed lunch.
I stood up there on the first day and
dug my hands into my pockets, thinking I
could hide my heart and its waywardness.
I slumped my shoulders, faced
the blackboard, shouted from
behind the projection screen.
But wherever I stood, my heart sparked
like a disco ball, doing
its unmistakeable kaleidoscope dance.
I went to my supervisor: I'm so
embarrassed, I said. I think my students
are judging me harshly. They've probably
never seen such a heart before.
She shuffled papers, looked at
the results of my classroom observation.
She said, Well, the best you can do
is be a role model. Maybe they've never had the chance to

learn about the heart. Try teaching it
the same way you teach grammar.
So I went back to class, and returned to
the living pulse of the text:
I glimpsed the luminous globe behind
the poem's dark ribs, felt its warmth streaming
through form, through syntax, through meter's
tangled orchard. I saw the poem as a latticework
interwoven with sun. Each sentence was
parsed by the light.
On the desks we drummed
the heartbeat of the iambs. My heart led an
orchestra of small flowers.

*Reminded me of my early days, when I assumed the children
could sense my nerves, knew when I made a mistake and could
tell that I would beat myself up when they left. Then when I
started to be me and not someone else teaching, it got easier,
just like this.*

Richard, primary teacher, West Lothian

INSTRUCTIONS ON NOT GIVING UP *Ada Limón*

More than the fuchsia funnels breaking out
of the crabapple tree, more than the neighbor's
almost obscene display of cherry limbs shoving
their cotton candy-colored blossoms to the slate
sky of Spring rains, it's the greening of the trees
that really gets to me. When all the shock of white
and taffy, the world's baubles and trinkets, leave
the pavement strewn with the confetti of aftermath,
the leaves come. Patient, plodding, a green skin
growing over whatever winter did to us, a return
to the strange idea of continuous living despite
the mess of us, the hurt, the empty. Fine then,
I'll take it, the tree seems to say, a new slick leaf
unfurling like a fist to an open palm, I'll take it all.

II

GETTING TO KNOW

FIRST DAY AT SCHOOL *Roger McGough*

A millionbillionwillion miles from home
waiting for the bell to go. (To go where?)
Why are they all so big, other children?
So noisy? So much at home they
must have been born in uniform.
Lived all their lives in playgrounds.
Spent the years inventing games
that don't let me in. Games
that are rough, that swallow you up.

And the railings.
All around, the railings.
Are they to keep out wolves and monsters?
Things that carry off and eat children?
Things you don't take sweets from?
Perhaps they're to stop us getting out.
Running away from the lessins. Lessin.
What does a lessin look like?
Sounds small and slimy.
They keep them in glassrooms.
Whole rooms made out of glass. Imagine.

I wish I could remember my name.
Mummy said it would come in useful.
Like wellies. When there's puddles.
Yellowwellies. I wish she was here.

I think my name is sewn on somewhere.
Perhaps the teacher will read it for me.
Tea-cher. The one who makes the tea.

The world should be an exciting safe place for a child experiencing new sights, smells and sounds but this poem reminds me that it can also be confusing and lonely. How I want to protect him and alleviate his fears!

Moira, recently retired Maths teacher

ISN'T MY NAME MAGICAL? *James Berry*

Nobody can see my name on me.
My name is inside
and all over me, unseen
like other people also keep it.
Isn't my name magical?

My name is mine only.
It tells I am individual,
the one special person it shakes
when I'm wanted.

Even if someone else answers
for me, my message hangs in air
haunting others, till it stops
with me, the right name.
Isn't your name and my name magic?

If I'm with hundreds of people
and my name gets called,
my sound switches me on to answer
like it was my human electricity.

My name echoes across playground
it comes, it demands my attention.
I have to find out who calls,
who wants me for what.
My name gets blurted out in class,

it is terror, at a bad time,
because somebody is cross.

My name gets called in a whisper
I am happy, because
my name may have touched me
with a loving voice.
Isn't your name and my name magic?

A BOY'S HEAD *Miroslav Holub*

In it there is a space-ship
and a project
for doing away with piano lessons.

And there is
Noah's ark,
which shall be first.

And there is
an entirely new bird,
an entirely new hare,
an entirely new bumble-bee.

There is a river
that flows upwards.

There is a multiplication table.

There is anti-matter.

And it just cannot be trimmed.

I believe
that only what cannot be trimmed
is a head.

There is much promise
in the circumstance
that so many people have heads.

SLOW READER *Vicki Feaver*

He can make a sculpture
and fabulous machines,
invent games, tell jokes,
give solemn, adult advice—
but he is slow to read.
When I take him on my knee
with his Ladybird book
he gazes into the air,
sighing and shaking his head
like an old man
who knows the mountains
are impassable.

He toys with words,
letting them go cold
as gristly meat,
until I relent
and let him wriggle free:
a fish returning
to its element,
or a white-eyed colt—shying
from the bit—who sees
that if he takes it
in his mouth
he'll never run
quite free again.

CLANN A CLUICH, SGOIL ACHADH NAN SIAN /
CHILDREN PLAYING, ACHNASHEEN SCHOOL

aonghas macneacail

glac am ball seo
tha saoghal ann

catch this ball
there's a world in it

cumaidh mise
mo shaoghal dlùth rium

I'll keep
my world close to me

tha mise cunntas nan saoghal
am barraibh mo mheòir

I'm counting the worlds
in the tips of my fingers

ni mise sgàirt agus
dannsa tromh'n àile
tha do chruinne gun fheum dhomh

I'll shout, and
dance through the air,
I don't need your globe

tha fàinne nam dhòrnsa, ach
có dh'iarradh fàinne

I clutch a ring, but
who needs a ring

eadar dàghreim tha ròpa
nathair nan cleas
nathair nan briathar
nathair nan òran

two hands hold a rope
the snake of games
the snake of words
the snake of songs

ON TURNING TEN   *Billy Collins*

The whole idea of it makes me feel
like I'm coming down with something,
something worse than any stomach ache
or the headaches I get from reading in bad light—
a kind of measles of the spirit,
a mumps of the psyche,
a disfiguring chicken pox of the soul.

You tell me it is too early to be looking back,
but that is because you have forgotten
the perfect simplicity of being one
and the beautiful complexity introduced by two.
But I can lie on my bed and remember every digit.
At four I was an Arabian wizard.
I could make myself invisible
by drinking a glass of milk a certain way.
At seven I was a soldier, at nine a prince.

But now I am mostly at the window
watching the late afternoon light.
Back then it never fell so solemnly
against the side of my tree house,
and my bicycle never leaned against the garage
as it does today,
all the dark blue speed drained out of it.

This is the beginning of sadness, I say to myself,
as I walk through the universe in my sneakers.
It is time to say good-bye to my imaginary friends,
time to turn the first big number.

It seems only yesterday I used to believe
there was nothing under my skin but light.
If you cut me I could shine.
But now when I fall upon the sidewalks of life,
I skin my knees. I bleed.

ARITHMETIC *Gavin Ewart*

I'm 11. And I don't really know
my Two Times Table. Teacher says it's disgraceful
but even if I had the time, I feel too tired.
Ron's 5, Samantha's 3, Carole's 18 months,
and then there's Baby. I do what's required.

Mum's working. Dad's away. And so
I dress them, give them breakfast. Mrs Russell
moves in, and I take Ron to school.
Miss Eames call me an old-fashioned word: Dunce.
Doreen Maloney says I'm a fool.

After tea, to the Rec. Pram-pushing's slow
but on fine days it's a good place, full
of larky boys. When 6 shows on the clock
I put the kids to bed. I'm free for once.
At about 7—Mum's key in the lock.

LOVE OF ALGEBRA *Eveline Pye*

She says, "You know how you get it
and then you forget it", and I smile,
nod—but really, I don't—
can't even imagine. How does
the dancer forget dancing,
the singer forget singing? How could
I ever not know how to solve
simultaneous equations?
It would be like forgetting
how to breathe or laugh or love.
You'd have to dissect my brain
scour out layer after layer of tissue
with steel wool, and even then
if you left me one tiny cell,
the knowledge would grow back,
and if you were to succeed,
to wipe out every trace,

                    I'd be a lost soul.
I'd never give up. I'd chew on my pencil
night and day to recapture that feeling,
that moment when I grasped the life line.

GLENIS *Allan Ahlberg*

The teacher says:

Why is it, Glenis,
Please answer me this,
The only time
You ever stop talking in class
Is if I ask you
Where's the Khyber Pass ?
Or when was the Battle of Waterloo?
Or what is nine times three?
Or how do you spell
Mississippi?
Why is it, Glenis,
The only time you are silent
Is when I ask you a question?

And Glenis says:

NO *Mark Doty*

The children have brought their wood turtle
into the dining hall
because they want us to feel

the power they have
when they hold a house
in their own hands, want us to feel

alien lacquer and the little thrill
that he might, like God, show his face.
He's the color of ruined wallpaper,

of cognac, and he's closed,
pulled in as though he'll never come out;
nothing shows but the plummy leather

of the legs, his claws resembling clusters
of diminutive raspberries.
They know he makes night

anytime he wants, so perhaps
he feels at the center of everything,
as they do. His age,

greater than that of anyone
around the table, is a room
from which they are excluded,

though they don't mind,
since they can carry this perfect
building anywhere. They love

that he might poke out
his old, old face, but doesn't.
I think the children smell unopened,

like unlit candles, as they heft him
around the table, praise his secrecy,
holding to each adult face

his prayer,
the single word of the shell,
which is no.

"O'm finking," says Hamid.
It's "I'm thinking," says the teacher.
"Nah man, that's wot you say 'cos you're a teacher
an' you're midoo class, but O'm not so I sez O'm finking.
It's like you goin' on about da geezer wrote
da macbef play, yeh. You sez to us, you sez,
"Don't get put off by da crappy langwidge,
'cos it's changin' alla time—da macbef langwidge
is like word-up on the street back then.
So wot I is sayin is O'm finkin, an' you
'ave to go along wiv dat 'cos it's the langwidge
changin', innit?"

DO' CARE *Bashabi Fraser*

In a Paris hotel lounge on one occasion
My thirteen year old five foot five
Daughter glowed with the attention
Of three young men striving
To pigeon-hole her Scottishness
And break her brittle brusqueness
With their far-eastern finesse.

If Scotland played England
Whom would she support
—Sco'land—was the answer delivered
And if England played India
—India—she claimed with a triumphant swagger
If England played Germany
—Germany—was the response
From the unassailable position
Of a new-found nationalism.

And what if it were Scotland and India
One demanded with the diabolical confidence
Of an argument-winning lawyer—
She clamped down her glass, shrugged her bare
Shoulders, turned away saying—do' care.

SAM BUT DIFFERENT *Christine De Luca*

Sam but different

Ha'in, fae da start, mair as ee wye o spaekin,
o makkin sense o things, we learn ta fit
whit we say ta whit's lippened. Takk pity apö dem
at's born ta wan tongue: dem at nivver preeve
maet fae idder tables. Raised wi twa languages
is unconscious faestin: twa wyes o tinkin.
Een extends da tidder; can shaa wis anidder wirld
yet foo aa wirlds ir jöst da sam, but different.

Same but different

Having, from the start, more than one way of speaking,
of making sense of things, we learn to fit
what we say to what's expected. Take pity on those
born to one tongue: those who never taste even a morsel
from other tables. Raised with two languages
is unconscious feasting: two ways of thinking.
One extends the other; can show us another world
yet how all worlds are just the same, but different.

PEOPLE EQUAL *James Berry*

Some people shoot up tall.
Some hardly leave the ground at all.
   Yet—people equal. Equal.

One voice is a sweet mango.
Another is a non-sugar tomato.
   Yet—people equal. Equal.

Some people rush to the front.
Others hang back, feeling they can't.
   Yet—people equal. Equal.

Hammer some people, you meet a wall
   Blow hard on others they fall.
   Yet—people equal. Equal.

One person will aim at a star.
   For another, a hilltop is *too far*.
   Yet—people equal. Equal.

Some people get on with their show.
Others never get on the go.
   Yet—people equal. Equal.

MY VOICE *Partaw Naderi*

صدا

من از سر زمین غریب می آیم
باکوله بار بیگانه گی ام بر دوش
و سرود خاموشی ام برلب
من یونس صدایم را
آن گاه که از رودبار حادثه می گذشتم
دیدم

درکامی نهنگی فرورفت
و تمام هستی من
در صدایم بود

شهرکابل
دسامبر ۱۹۸۹

My Voice

I come from a distant land
with a foreign knapsack on my back
with a silenced song on my lips

As I travelled down the river of my life
I saw my voice
(like Jonah)
swallowed by a whale

And my very life lived in my voice

trans from the Farsi-Dari by Sarah Maguire *and* Yama Yari

A BOOK CLOSER TO HOME *Nabila Jameel*

Every Saturday mum took us to the library.
We dispersed into different parts of the room,

craving this yellow smell of bound paper
and a peep into lives we did not live—
where tea was not chai, but dinner.

Mum sat in the Urdu section,
soon dissolving into a magazine
full of squiggles that only made sense to her.

Her large almond eyes smiled.
Her soft fingers turned the pages,
pausing while she glanced at us with motherly duty.

We sat with our books on the carpeted floor,
following the curves and lines of English
with our fingertips,

the red signs on the mahogany shelves
silencing our tongue.

CLASSROOM POLITICS *Fiona Norris*

They will not forgive us
These girls
Sitting in serried rows
Hungry for attention
Like shelves of unread books
If we do not
Make the world new for them
Teach them to walk
Into the possibilities
Of their own becoming
Confident in their exploring.

They will not forget
If we do not use
Our often-surrendered positions
On the front line
To wage war against
The subtle hordes of male historians
Who constantly edit female experience
And endlessly anthologise
Their own achievements.

They will not accept
The old excuses of their foremothers
If they grow up to find
That we have betrayed them.

DUNCAN GETS EXPELLED *Jackie Kay*

There are three big boys from primary seven
who wait at the main school gate with stones
in their teeth and names in their pockets.
Every day the three big boys are waiting.
'There she is. Into her, boys. Hey, Sambo.'

I dread the bell ringing, and the walk home.
My best friend is scared of them and runs off.
Some days they shove a mud pie into my mouth.
'That's what you should eat,' and make me eat it.
Then they all look into my mouth, prodding a stick.

I'm always hoping we get detention.
I'd love to write 'I will be better' 400 times.
The things I do? I pull Agnes MacNamara's hair.
Or put a ruler under Rhona's bum and ping it back
till she screams; or I make myself sick in the toilet.

Until the day the headmaster pulls me out,
asking all about the three big boys.
I'm scared to open my mouth.
But he says, 'You can tell me, is it true?'
So out it comes, making me eat the mud pies.

Two of them got lines for the whole of May.
But he got expelled, that Duncan MacKay.

LISTEN *Liz Lochhead*

*Written for the Children's Panel, to encourage
new voluntary members, 2012.*

Trouble is not my middle name.
It is not what I am.
I was not born for this.
Trouble is not a place
though I am in it deeper than the deepest wood
and I'd get out of it (who wouldn't?) if I could.

Hope is what I do not have in hell—
not without good help, now. Could you
listen, listen hard and well
to what I cannot say except by what I do?

And when you say I do it for badness
this much is true:
I do it for badness done to me before
any badness that I do to you.

Hard to unfankle this.
But you can help me.
Maybe.
Loosen
all these knots and really listen.
I cannot plainly tell you this, but, if you care,
then—beyond all harm and hurt—
real hope is there.

YOUR DAD DID WHAT? *Sophie Hannah*

Where they have been, if they have been away,
or what they've done at home, if they have not—
you make them write about the holiday.
One writes *My Dad did*. What? Your Dad did what?

That's not a sentence. Never mind the bell.
We stay behind until the work is done.
You count their words (you who can count and spell);
all the assignments are complete bar one

and though this boy seems bright, that one is his.
He says he's finished, doesn't want to add
anything, hands it in just as it is.
No change. *My Dad did*. What? What did his Dad?

You find the 'E' you gave him as you sort
through reams of what this girl did, what that lad did,
and read the line again, just one 'e' short:
This holiday was horrible. My Dad did.

This simple, beautiful poem captures the poignancy, experienced all too often in teaching, of clarity when we glimpse the real lives of our children and young people, in school for just 16% of the hours of their school-age lives.

Angela Bell, DHT Secondary

THE SACRED *Stephen Dunn*

After the teacher asked if anyone had
  a sacred place
and the students fidgeted and shrunk

in their chairs, the most serious of them all
  said it was his car,
being in it alone, his tape deck playing

things he'd chosen, and others knew the truth
  had been spoken
and began speaking about their rooms,

their hiding places, but the car kept coming
  up, the car in motion,
music filling it, and sometimes one other person

who understood the bright altar of the dashboard
  and how far away
a car could take him from the need

to speak, or to answer, the key
  in having a key
and putting it in, and going.

EVERY LINE IS IMAGINARY *William Letford*

A jumble of bodies bobbing and shifting.
There is sweat, and rhythm, and pain.
One turn from the end.
He is last.
I wish he already knew
that finishing lines don't really exist,
that the trick is not stopping.
But he is twelve years old,
full of summer
and, would you believe it, coming up fast.

SCAFFOLDING *Eveline Pye*

They need to trust you
describe their reasoning
in detail. Each premise
must be laid bare.

"Why did you do that?

Where did *that* number
come from?"

I follow each step
searching for the wrong idea
the mistaken concept.

Sometimes, all I gift
is one new thought like...
"Dividing *can* make
a number bigger"
and it's as if I see
their minds inflate.

It's like blowing air
into someone else's lungs.
You have to stop
as soon as you can.

You need them
to breathe again
—all on their own.

*'I see their minds inflate' —a line that wonderfully summed
up those fleeting and always to be savoured moments when you
can see the children learn. That's why we teach, not to go to
meetings but to help them all grow.*

Richard, primary teacher, West Lothian

THE DOMINIE'S ANNUAL IMPROVEMENT PLAN

William Hershaw

The Curriculum:
Aa the stuff
the bairns
hivtae ken.

Meeting Learners' Needs:
Helpin the bairns
hou tae lairn
aa the stuff.

Improving Learners' Experiences:
The bairns haein
a braw time
lairnin aa the stuff.

Improvements in Performance:
The bairns daein weill
at mindin
aa the stuff.

Improvements Through Self-Evaluation:
Tae see oursels
as the bairns see us
teaching them aa the stuff.

III

BALANCING IT ALL

INTRODUCTION TO POETRY *Billy Collins*

I ask them to take a poem
and hold it up to the light
like a color slide

or press an ear against its hive.

I say drop a mouse into a poem
and watch him probe his way out,

or walk inside the poem's room
and feel the walls for a light switch.

I want them to waterski
across the surface of a poem
waving at the author's name on the shore.

But all they want to do
is tie the poem to a chair with rope
and torture a confession out of it.

They begin beating it with a hose
to find out what it really means.

*This poem made me, as a former English teacher, smile. I liked
its humorous contrast of the teaching of a delicate appreciation*

*of poetry and all its nuance, with the temptation to resort
to brutal, joyless over-analysis of it in pursuit of 'the correct
answer'. Encouraging our students to look, listen and feel their
way to understanding poems and the thoughts and emotions
that their authors might have been trying to stir in us, boosts
their enjoyment of poetry—both reading it and writing it.*

Andrea Bradley, **former secondary teacher**

DID I MISS ANYTHING? *Tom Wayman*

Nothing. When we realized you weren't here
we sat with our hands folded on our desks
in silence, for the full two hours

    Everything. I gave an exam worth
    40 per cent of the grade for this term
    and assigned some reading due today
    on which I'm about to hand out a quiz
    worth 50 per cent

Nothing. None of the content of this course
has value or meaning
Take as many days off as you like:
any activities we undertake as a class
I assure you will not matter either to you or me
and are without purpose

    Everything. A few minutes after we began last time
    a shaft of light suddenly descended and an angel
    or other heavenly being appeared
    and revealed to us what each woman or man must do
    to attain divine wisdom in this life and
    the hereafter
    This is the last time the class will meet
    before we disperse to bring the good news to all people on earth.

Nothing. When you are not present
how could something significant occur?

Everything. Contained in this classroom
is a microcosm of human experience
assembled for you to query and examine and ponder
This is not the only place such an opportunity has been gathered

but it was one place

And you weren't here

'What did I miss?' wouldn't have stung so much, would it?
So, this wildly-exaggerated (unspoken) frustration is not
directed at the pupil asking for help to catch up after absence;
it's laughing away our own frustration, teasing ourselves for
letting that casual wording hit a raw nerve.

Jane Cooper, secondary teacher, Edinburgh

FOUR A.M. *Wisława Szymborska*

The hour between night and day.
The hour between toss and turn.
The hour of thirty-year-olds.

The hour swept clean for roosters' crowing.
The hour when the earth takes back its warm embrace.
The hour of cool drafts from extinguished stars.
The hour of do-we-vanish-too-without-a-trace.

Empty hour.
Hollow. Vain.
Rock bottom of all the other hours.

No one feels fine at four a.m.
If ants feel fine at four a.m.,
we're happy for the ants. And let five a.m. come
if we've got to go on living.

*Translated from Polish by Stanisław Barańczak
and Clare Cavanagh*

SOMETIMES *Anon*

Sometimes things don't go, after all,
from bad to worse. Some years, muscadel
faces down frost; green thrives; the crops don't fail,
sometimes a man aims high, and all goes well.

A people sometimes will step back from war;
elect an honest man; decide they care
enough, that they can't leave some stranger poor.
Some men become what they are born for.

Sometimes our best efforts do not go
amiss; sometimes we do as we meant to.
The sun will sometimes melt a field of sorrow
that seemed hard frozen: may it happen for you.

THE PEACE OF WILD THINGS *Wendell Berry*

When despair for the world grows in me
and I wake in the night at the least sound
in fear of what my life and my children's lives may be,
I go and lie down where the wood drake
rests in his beauty on the water, and the great heron feeds.
I come into the peace of wild things
who do not tax their lives with forethought
of grief. I come into the presence of still water.
And I feel above me the day-blind stars
waiting with their light. For a time
I rest in the grace of the world, and am free.

SCHOOL AT FOUR O'CLOCK *Charles Causley*

At four o'clock the building enters harbour.
All day it seems that we have been at sea.
Now, having lurched through the last of the water,
We lie, stone-safe, beside the jumping quay.
The stiff waves propped against the classroom window,
The razor-back of cliffs we never pass,
The question-mark of green coiling behind us,
Have all turned into cabbages, slates, grass.

Up the slow hill a squabble of children wanders
As silence dries the valley like a drought,
When suddenly that speechless cry is raging
Once more round these four walls to be let out.
Like playing cards the Delabole slates flutter,
The founding stone is shaken in its mine,
The faultless evening light begins to stutter
As the cry hurtles down the chimney-spine.

Packing my bag with useless bits of paper
I wonder, when the last word has been said,
If I'd prefer to find each sound was thudding
Not round the school, but just inside my head.
I watch where the street lamp with sodium finger
Touches the darkening voices as they fall.
Outside? Inside? Perhaps either condition's
Better than his who hears nothing at all.

And I recall another voice. A teacher
Long years ago, saying, *I think I know*
Where all the children come from, but the puzzle
To me is, as they grow up, where they go?
Love, wonder, marvellous hope. All these can wither
With crawling years like flowers on a stalk;
Or, to some Piper's tune, vanish for ever
As creatures murdered on a morning walk.

Though men may blow this building up with powder,
Drag its stone guts to knacker's yard, or tip,
Smash its huge heart to dust, and spread the shingle
By the strong sea, or sink it like a ship—
Listen. Through the clear shell of air the voices
Still strike like water from the mountain bed;
The cry of those who to a certain valley
Hungry and innocent came. And were not fed.

END OF YEAR EXAM *Hugh McMillan*

A floorboard creaks
but mostly it's like the sea,
old grain flowing like dark water.
Overhead, through tall windows,
the breeze catches clouds.
It is a voyage this, just the beginning,
but they are moving away,
sails are filling,
they are beating time on paper with ink,
the destination a dream,
the impetus all that matters,
the keel dragging free of shale.

LEAVING TEACHING *Kim Moore*

When I walk into Year 3 each Tuesday morning
they always have their mouthpieces in their hands.
Who would like to buzz I say and we begin,
back and forward, call and response.
Let's pretend we're on a motorbike.
Let's pretend we are bees.
At the end, one of the girls hugs me and says
I'm really glad you're our music teacher,
and a boy says *where did you get your shoes from Miss,*
they're well cool, and I'll admit it, my heart soars a little
and the idea of leaving it behind in July,
of never having to pull a perfect B^b from the air
with my voice for the class to copy, no not the air,
after all these years, it feels as if that note lives
in my chest, I've carried it for so long, the idea
of never giving this to anyone again feels terrible.
Thank god for the afternoon session, when a girl
tells me she's bored, and a boy leans on his trumpet
then runs around it in a circle, so the mouthpiece gets stuck,
and the whole lesson feels like a battle, the class
talking through my recap of crotchets and minims,
although it's not the whole class, it's never the whole class,
just a constant few, talking their lives away,
whispering I don't know what, my mind can't
reach back across the years to think what it was
that we used to whisper behind our desks.
Today there was a fight at lunchtime and rudeness

to the dinner ladies, who come in outraged
and wanting retribution. I've been asked to save
the Year 5 end-of-term performance
of Joseph and the Amazing Technicolour Dreamcoat
which will involve gathering around the piano
and an explanation of the head and chest voice.
Two boys won't stop shoving each other as another
tells me over and over again *my valves are sticking,*
actually he says *my vowels are sticking,*
his hand waving in the air, *my vowels my vowels,*
my vowels are sticking and I admit it, I lose my temper
and give up all at the same time, it's like being a balloon
ready to burst and then being popped, it is a terrible thing,
this moving on, this giving in.

DEATH OF A TEACHER *Carol Ann Duffy*

The big trees outside are into their poker game again,
shuffling and dealing, turning, folding, their leaves

drifting down to the lawn, floating away, ace high,
on a breeze. You died yesterday.

When I heard the hour—home time, last bell,
late afternoon—I closed my eyes. English, of course,

three decades back, and me thirteen. You sat on your desk,
swinging your legs, reading a poem by Yeats

to the bored girls, except my heart stumbled and blushed
as it fell in love with the words and I saw the tree

in the scratched old desk under my hands, heard the bird
in the oak outside scribble itself on the air. We were truly there,

present, Miss, or later the smoke from your black cigarette
braided itself with lines from Keats. Teaching

is endless love; the poems by heart, spells, the lists
lovely on the learning tongue, the lessons, just as you said,

for life. Under the gambling trees, the gold light thins and burns, the edge of a page of a book, precious, waiting to be turned.

A few years ago a colleague and friend died after a short illness. We were all dressed sombrely on the morning of her funeral. One child wondered aloud where we were going. A colleague gently explained. "Oh," the child exclaimed, "is she the lady that was always happy and smiling?" We all agreed this was a fitting tribute and one which continues to influence us daily.

L. N., primary teacher, Edinburgh

CHANGED *Dave Calder*

For months he taught us, stiff-faced.
His old tweed jacket closely buttoned up,
his gestures careful and deliberate.

We didn't understand what he was teaching us.
It was as if a veil, a gauzy bandage, got between
what he was showing us and what we thought we saw.

He had the air of a gardener, fussily protective
of young seedlings, but we couldn't tell
if he was hiding something or we simply couldn't see it.

At first we noticed there were often scraps of leaves
on the floor where he had stood. Later, thin wisps
of thread like spider's web fell from his jacket.

Finally we grew to understand the work. And on that day
he opened his jacket, which to our surprise
seemed lined with patterned fabric of many shimmering hues.

Then he smiled and sighed. And with this movement
the lining rippled and instantly the room was filled
with a flickering storm of swirling butterflies.

RETIRING *Steven Herrick*

Our teacher, Mrs Batlow
is leaving this week,
after 40 years of teaching.
So on Friday all of Class 5W
give her a present.
Most of us give her a card
with *'best wishes'* but
Sarah presents her with a painting
of Mrs Batlow standing in front of the school.
Emily gives her some flowers.
Nathan gives her a box of chocolates.
Lorenzo gives her a framed photo of Class 5W.
Penny gives her a box of apples!
(Penny's Dad owns a fruit shop.)
Simon gives her a pen in a special case.
Mrs Batlow smiles at each present
and thanks every child
but when Peter gives her his homework
all finished, neat and tidy,
for the first time this year
we all notice that
Mrs Batlow is crying
but
we're not sure if she's happy
or
if she's crying because
she has to mark Peter's homework.

IV

NEW EVERY MORNING

from **NEW EVERY MORNING** *Susan Coolidge*

Every day is a fresh beginning;
  Listen, my soul, to the glad refrain,
And, spite of old sorrow and older sinning,
  And puzzles forecasted and possible pain,
  Take heart with the day, and begin again.

*It's hard when you have had a difficult day not to carry the
emotions through to the next one. The awkward pupil, the
failed lesson. Each day start fresh, a new page, a belief that
today you will make a difference...and when you do the
feeling is like no other.*

Mamaburns, recently retired primary teacher

SOME DAYS *David Harmer*

Some days this school
is a huge concrete sandwich
squeezing me out like jam.

It weighs so much
breathing hurts, my legs freeze
my body is heavy.

On days like that
I carry whole buildings
high on my back.

Other days
the school is a rocket
thrusting right into the sun.

It's yellow and green
freshly painted,
the cabin windows
gleam with laughter.

On days like that
whole buildings support me,
my ladder is pushing
over their rooftops.

Amongst the clouds
I'd need a computer
to count all the bubbles
bursting aloud in my head.

*Great stuff—to me this is what teaching is like! The
intensity and drama of the everyday, the frustration and
the stress—but oh, the fun and the satisfaction and
the elation!*

Primary teacher, Edinburgh

LEARNING *Kay Ryan*

Whatever must be learned
is always on the bottom,
as with the law of drawers
and the necessary item.
It isn't pleasant,
whatever they tell children,
to turn out on the floor
the folded things in them.

TWENTY BLESSINGS *Thomas A. Clark*

May the best hour of the day be yours.
May luck go with you from hill to sea.
May you stand against the prevailing wind.
May no forest intimidate you.
May you look out from your own eyes.
May near and far attend you.
May you bathe your face in the sun's rays.
May you have milk, cream, substance.
May your actions be effective.
May your thoughts be affective.
May you will both the wild and the mild.
May you sing the lark from the sky.
May you place yourself in circumstance.
May you be surrounded by goldfinches.
May you pause among alders.
May your desire be infinite.
May what you touch be touched.
May the company be less for your leaving.
May you walk alone beneath the stars.
May your embers still glow in the morning.

EVERYTHING IS GOING TO BE ALL RIGHT *Derek Mahon*

How should I not be glad to contemplate
the clouds clearing beyond the dormer window
and a high tide reflected on the ceiling?
There will be dying, there will be dying,
but there is no need to go into that.
The poems flow from the hand unbidden
and the hidden source is the watchful heart.
The sun rises in spite of everything
and the far cities are beautiful and bright.
I lie here in a riot of sunlight
watching the day break and the clouds flying.
Everything is going to be all right.

TO BE OF USE *Marge Piercy*

The people I love the best
jump into work head first
without dallying in the shallows
and swim off with sure strokes almost out of sight.
They seem to become natives of that element,
the black sleek heads of seals
bouncing like half-submerged balls.

I love people who harness themselves, an ox to a heavy cart,
who pull like water buffalo, with massive patience,
who strain in the mud and the muck to move things forward,
who do what has to be done, again and again.

I want to be with people who submerge
in the task, who go into the fields to harvest
and work in a row and pass the bags along,
who are not parlor generals and field deserters
but move in a common rhythm
when the food must come in or the fire be put out.

The work of the world is common as mud.
Botched, it smears the hands, crumbles to dust.
But the thing worth doing well done
has a shape that satisfies, clean and evident.
Greek amphoras for wine or oil,

Hopi vases that held corn, are put in museums
but you know they were made to be used.
The pitcher cries for water to carry
and a person for work that is real.

*Teaching offers no option but to jump in and be fully
submerged. You have to be so many things and take
many forms, but this is real work. With great reward.*

S.D., secondary teacher

PLATONIC DIALOGUE *Gregory Woods*

I speak you listen
you speak I listen
I ask you questions
you give me answers
I give you answers
I outline a fact
you repeat the fact
I outline a theory
you question the theory
I tell a laboured joke
you forgive with laughter
you tell a rude joke
I pretend to be shocked
I write on the board
you write in your notebook
I frown you frown
you smile I smile
you chew your pencil
you scratch your temple
I teach you learn
you learn I learn
I fall silent
you fall silent
I get bored with you
you get bored with me
I stifle a yawn
you stifle a laugh

I make you work
you make me work
you read what I've written
I read what you've written
I teach from experience
you learn by experience
I recite what I've memorized
you memorize what I recite
I want you to say it again
you want me to say it again
you learn by heart
I teach by heart
my voice in your ear
my words on your lips
I stay here you go there
your life is there
here your chewed pencil

The reciprocal nature of teaching is laid out beautifully here: the biggest successes are the students who surpass you. I often reassure students with "I'm not smarter than you, I've just had time to learn more."

Emma Grieve, secondary English teacher, Orkney

WHAT FIFTY SAID *Robert Frost*

When I was young my teachers were the old.
I gave up fire for form till I was cold.
I suffered like a metal being cast.
I went to school to age to learn the past.

Now I am old my teachers are the young.
What can't be molded must be cracked and sprung.
I strain at lessons fit to start a suture.
I go to school to youth to learn the future.

IN THIS SHORT LIFE *Emily Dickinson*

In this short Life
That only lasts an hour
How much—how little—is
Within our power

NOTES ABOUT THE POEMS

Dave Calder

I had been helping a child struggle with homework and got to thinking on the long process of learning, of the moment of "getting it", of the satisfaction and release at reaching that understanding to both pupil and teacher—like something growing and hatching, I thought…

Thomas A. Clark

In traditional societies it was a common practice to offer blessings and short prayers on almost any occasion, for the success of the occasion or for the well-being of the company. A few lines of 'Twenty Blessings' are taken directly from the *Carmina Gadelica*, a collection of material from the Gaelic oral tradition.

Vicki Feaver

This poem, one of the first I ever wrote, was about my son. The Ladybird book was the reader he brought home from his primary school. A couple of months later he was given a book that really excited him and he was soon reading fluently on his own. For me the poem is partly about a child who has been put off reading by finding books rather dull; partly about the feeling that a child, like a colt, needs to run free for a time and enjoy themselves.

It was also, I think, a bit about me. I was a 'slow poet'. I wanted to be a poet as a child but didn't have the courage to write until I was in my mid thirties.

Rebecca Lynne Fullan

I wrote this poem after my first year of teaching. During that year, I felt like I was failing every time I walked in the classroom. About halfway through, I realized that failure, in terms of being pushed out beyond what I knew confidently, was the condition of teaching well.

David Harmer

I wrote this poem quite a long time ago when I was a primary school teacher. I knew that for some of the children school wasn't great some days, and on other days it was really exciting! I also knew that it was the same for me and teachers everywhere. We all bring stuff in our heads to school which can make it a bad day but very often being with our friends and doing things we really like can make going to school fantastic. In fact, most days it is like that.

But on some days...

Steven Herrick

When my sons were children, each afternoon they would eagerly tell me about their school day. They knew I'd turn their memories into poems. They were generous in allowing a house-bound poet to leave his desk and wander with them through the classroom and schoolyard. It was the best journey of my life.

Nabila Jameel

This poem has emerged from my weekly visits on a Saturday to the local library with my mum. It addresses the idea of 'woman' before 'mother', the loss of language, the finding of peace and contentment in the written form of the mother tongue; and the harsh dominance of the superior language.

Maggie Kazel

My first year gave me such a wake up call—realizing I loved kids and teaching. But being lesbian there in such a 'straight' environment was almost too much. A veteran teacher—Terri—was my unofficial mentor. Sharing my fear with him broke my paralyzing silence—all new teachers deserve their own Terri.

William Letford

I'd watched my nephew racing for his school. I felt I was running with him. It reminded me of all the finishing lines, deadlines, aims, targets, and goals that had risen up and fallen away. How important they seem and insignificant they become. I wanted to shout, keep going, you'll be okay.

Liz Lochhead

Glad this poem has been chosen for this anthology because teachers will I hope recognise and empathise with the speaker of the poem. A boy of about 14 or 15, I think—though could be a particularly sullen and troubled girl? Seems everyone needs reminding that the 'I' speaking a poem is not necessarily the poet. I've always enjoyed using 'impoverished' clichés in a playful way because I love listening to colloquial speech. The irony is, this silent, or silenced, voice is only able to articulate itself within the impossible world of the poem.

Christine De Luca

Growing up bilingual—Shetlandic and English—I gradually came to appreciate the joys of linguistic flexibility. Languages open doors into apparently different worlds, but stepping further in, the differences fade away in our common humanity. I try to help children value their mother tongue but also to enjoy learning other languages.

Aonghas Macneacail

As a writer, I have visited many schools. Each is, in its own way, a means of rediscovering your own childhood, into which the experiences of all the intervening years may be fed. The essence is to revisit and marry that knowledge with a retained sense of innocence.

Rowland Molony

How to tackle Shakespeare in school? 'Hamid' is a brief look at the gap between young people and 400-year-old Shakespeare. Shakespeare has cracking stories and magnetic characters. In teaching him, story is primary, language secondary. First get into the drama, then the brilliance of the words.

Fiona Norris

'Classroom Politics' was written way back in the early 1980s when I was a young English teacher, keen to make a real difference to my pupils, both in their learning and in their lives. This simple poem expresses the sense of responsibility I felt, particularly towards the girls.

Nina Pick

I wrote this poem when I was struggling with my role as a teacher in a university, higher education in general being a place where intellectualism is privileged and embodiment and intuition—more feminine ways of knowing—are discounted. I was just learning how to stand in front of a classroom as a shy person, as a person with a body, and be authentic, rather than hide behind a mask or a persona. I ultimately came to the decision that I wanted to model a kind of honesty or integrity to my students, that a way of being could also be way of teaching.

Gregory Woods
I taught in universities. My career began with plenty of work in personal tutorials and small seminar groups. It ended with distance-learning packs and lectures to crowds of people who weren't necessarily even in the same room. Teaching should be an intimate conversation, with love and respect on both sides.

ACKNOWLEDGEMENTS

Allan Ahlberg, 'Glenis', from *Please Mrs Butler* (Puffin, 2013), copyright © Allan Ahlberg, 1984, reproduced by permission of Penguin Books Ltd; James Berry, 'Isn't My Name Magical' and 'People Equal' from *A Story I Am In: Selected Poems* (Bloodaxe Books, 2011), reproduced with permission of Bloodaxe Books, www.bloodaxebooks.com; Wendell Berry, 'The Peace of Wild Things', from *New Collected Poems*, copyright © 2012 by Wendell Berry. Reprinted by permission of Counterpoint Press; Dave Calder, 'Changed', from *Dolphins Leap Lampposts* (Macmillan Children's, 2002), by permission of the author; Charles Causley, 'School at Four O'Clock' from *Collected Poems 1951–2000* (Macmillan), by permission of David Higham Associates; Thomas A. Clark, 'Twenty Blessings' (Moschatel Press, 1999), by permission of the author; Billy Collins, 'On Turning Ten', from *The Art of Drowning* and 'Introduction to Poetry', from *The Apple That Astonished Paris* (1988), by permission of Chris Calhoun Agency LLC on behalf of the author; Christine De Luca, 'Sam But Different / Same But Different', by permission of the author; Emily Dickinson, 'In this short life', from *The Poems Of Emily Dickinson*, edited by Thomas H. Johnson, Cambridge, Mass.: The Belknap Press of Harvard University Press, Copyright © 1951, 1955 by the President and Fellows of Harvard College. Copyright © renewed 1979, 1983 by the President and Fellows of Harvard College. Copyright © 1914, 1918, 1919, 1924, 1929, 1930, 1932, 1935, 1937, 1942, by Martha Dickinson Bianchi. Copyright © 1952, 1957, 1958, 1963, 1965, by Mary L. Hampson; Mark Doty, 'No', from *My Alexandria*, copyright 1993 Mark Doty. Used with permission of the University of Illinois Press; Carol Ann Duffy, 'Death of a Teacher' from *New Selected Poems*

Eveline Pye, 'Love of Algebra' and 'Scaffolding', by permission of the author; Kay Ryan, 'Learning', from *Odd Blocks: Selected and New Poems* (Carcanet Press, 2011), by permission of the publisher; Wisława Szymborska, 'Four A.M.' from *Poems New And Collected 1957–1997*, translated from the Polish by Stanisław Barańczak and Clare Cavanagh. English translation copyright © 1998 by Houghton Mifflin Harcourt Publishing Company. Used by permission of Houghton Mifflin Harcourt Publishing Company; Gael Turnbull, 'Lines for a Bookmark' from *There Are Words: Collected Poems* (Shearsman Books, 2006), by permission of Jill Turnbull; Tom Wayman, 'Did I Miss Anything?' from *Did I Miss Anything? Selected Poems 1973–1993* (Harbour Publishing, 1993); Gregory Woods, 'Platonic Dialogue', by permission of the author. We are glad to have permission to reproduce 'Sometimes'.

*

With thanks to the teachers, including those named here, who helped us choose poems:

Gregor Addison, FE communications lecturer, West Dunbartonshire · Clare Bethell, STEM coordinator, North Ayrshire · Isabel Braadbaart, primary teacher, Aberdeenshire · Michelle Bradley, secondary teacher of English, City of Edinburgh · Lynn Davidson, secondary teacher of Geography, North Ayrshire · Lauren Doherty, secondary teacher of History, Dumfries and Galloway · Lauren McDaid, secondary teacher of English, Dumfries and Galloway · Jennifer Elstone, primary teacher, North Ayrshire · Elsbeth Helfer, primary teacher, Fife · Margaret Higgins, FE communications lecturer, West Dunbartonshire · Ròs Hunter, secondary teacher of Science and

Biology, City of Edinburgh · Evelyn Love-Gajardo, Development Officer: Literacy Strategy, City of Edinburgh Council · Moira Scott, newly-retired secondary teacher of Maths, City of Edinburgh · Claire Smail, Literacy Development Officer, City of Edinburgh · Keith Walker, still-enthusiastic veteran STEM teacher, Dumfries and Galloway · Ourania Varsou, Lecturer, University of St Andrews.

With thanks to all the teachers who wrote in response to particular poems. We had difficulty picking just a few for the book, but we selected comments written by:

Andrea Bradley, former secondary teacher · Angela Bell, DHT Secondary · Emma Grieve, secondary English teacher, Orkney · Ernesto L. Abeytia, poet and writer, university-level literature, writing and film, USA · L. N., primary teacher, Edinburgh · Mamaburns, recently retired primary teacher, Moray · Moira, recently-retired Maths teacher · Primary teacher, Edinburgh · Richard, primary teacher, West Lothian · S. D., secondary teacher.

THE SCOTTISH POETRY LIBRARY
Bringing people and poems together

Our Scottish and international collections are housed just off Edinburgh's Royal Mile, in the UK's only purpose-built poetry library. Even if you can't get to the building, you can explore our resources on poetry and creative learning at: www.scottishpoetrylibrary.org.uk

We'd love to hear your thoughts on this book. Email us at: poemsforteachers@spl.org.uk

THE GENERAL TEACHING COUNCIL FOR SCOTLAND

Assuring and enhancing educational professionalism; inspiring world-class learning and teaching

The General Teaching Council for Scotland (GTCS) is the independent professional body which maintains and enhances teaching standards and promotes and regulates the teaching profession in Scotland.

www.gtcs.org.uk

EDUCATIONAL INSTITUTE OF SCOTLAND

Scotland's largest and most effective education trade union

The Educational Institute of Scotland (EIS) is the largest teaching union in Scotland, and the oldest in the world. The EIS represents and supports over 80% of Scotland's teaching professionals at all career levels across nursery, primary, secondary, special, further and higher education.

www.eis.org.uk

AHDS

Representing school leaders

AHDS is a professional association supporting and representing promoted teachers in Scotland's primary, nursery and ASN schools. We hope this book is interesting to you throughout your teaching journey. If you move into management, here's where to find us:

www.ahds.org.uk

NASUWT

The teachers' union

NASUWT is the fastest growing teachers' union in Scotland, representing teachers and head teachers from early years to further education. NASUWT has secured significant improvements in pay and working conditions for teachers. Legal and professional services are provided by a network of national, regional and local offices.

www.nasuwt.org.uk/advice/scotland.html

SCOTTISH SECONDARY TEACHERS' ASSOCIATION

Scotland's specialist union for secondary teachers

The Scottish Secondary Teachers' Association (SSTA) is Scotland's only specialist union for Secondary Teachers. Founded in 1944, the SSTA was set up to focus on secondary issues with a commitment to ensure that the secondary view is properly represented.

www.ssta.org.uk